Faro
Travel Guide

Quick Trips Series

No part of this publication may be reproduced, stored in a retrieval system, or transmitted, in any form or by any means without the prior written permission of the publisher, nor be otherwise circulated in any form of binding or cover other than that in which it is published and without similar condition being imposed on the subsequent purchaser. If there are any errors or omissions in copyright acknowledgements the publisher will be pleased to insert the appropriate acknowledgement in any subsequent printing of this publication. Although we have taken all reasonable care in researching this book we make no warranty about the accuracy or completeness of its content and disclaim all liability arising from its use.

Copyright © 2016, Astute Press
All Rights Reserved.

Table of Contents

FARO 6

- ◉ CUSTOMS & CULTURE 10
- ◉ GEOGRAPHY 11
- ◉ WEATHER & BEST TIME TO VISIT 13
- ◉ MONEY & CURRENCY 14
- ◉ MAPS 15

SIGHTS & ACTIVITIES: WHAT TO SEE & DO 16

- ◉ OLD TOWN 16
  - Arco de Vila 18
  - Cathedral 18
  - Bishop's Palace 20
  - Municipal Museum of Archeology 21
- ◉ RIA FORMOSA NATURE PARK 22
- ◉ OUR LADY OF CARMEL CHURCH & CHAPEL OF BONES 24
- ◉ BEACHES 25
  - Praia de Faro & Ilha de Faro 26
  - Ilha de Barreta/Deserta 26
  - Vale de Lobo 27
  - Armona 28
- ◉ LIVING SCIENCE CENTRE 28
- ◉ ESTOI & THE MILREU RUINS 29
- ◉ TAVIRA 31

Roman Bridge 31
Tavira Island 32
🌐 VILAMOURA **33**
Vilamoura Marina 34
Cerro da Vila 35

BUDGET TIPS   37

🌐 ACCOMMODATION 37
Casa d'Alagoa Hostel 37
Hotel Ibis Faro 38
Hotel Adelaide 39
Hotel Faro 40
Quinta dos Poetas, Hotel Rural Olhao 41

🌐 RESTAURANTS, CAFÉS & BARS 42
Columbus Cocktail and Wine Bar 42
Tasca do Ricky 43
Jamie's Faro 44
Adega Nova 44
Atelier de Comida Sto Antonio 45

🌐 SHOPPING 46
Forum Algarve 46
Mercado Municipal de Faro 47
Carminho 48
Garrafeira Rui 48
Estoi Flea Market 49

KNOW BEFORE YOU GO   50

🌐 ENTRY REQUIREMENTS 50
🌐 HEALTH INSURANCE 50
🌐 TRAVELLING WITH PETS 51
🌐 AIRPORTS 52
🌐 AIRLINES 53
🌐 CURRENCY 54

- Banking & ATMs 54
- Credit Cards 54
- Tourist Taxes 55
- Reclaiming VAT 55
- Tipping Policy 56
- Mobile Phones 56
- Dialling Code 57
- Emergency Numbers 57
- Public Holidays 58
- Time Zone 58
- Daylight Savings Time 59
- School Holidays 59
- Trading Hours 59
- Driving Laws 60
- Drinking Laws 61
- Smoking Laws 61
- Electricity 62
- Tourist Information (TI) 62
- Food & Drink 63
- Websites 64

FARO TRAVEL GUIDE

Faro

Mainland Portugal's southernmost city, scenic Faro is the capital of the Algarve. A colourful town marked by long sandy beaches and flanked by dramatic rocks. Born inside medieval walls, the city unfolds its long story; one of a mish-mash of influences and periods of both prominence and devastation.

FARO TRAVEL GUIDE

Unfortunately, most foreign sun-seekers are often whisked away to other parts of the region shortly upon arrival to Faro, with the town of 50,000 inhabitants serving as a main gateway to the wider Algarve area. By doing so, they are overlooking the surprising beauty that is Faro – endless sweeping beaches, a historic old town and a delightful National Park all on its doorstep, waiting to be explored.

The scenery in Faro is unlike what one finds elsewhere in Algarve, where steep cliffs, majestic rocks and wild waves dominate the landscape. Here, tranquil waters and white sands are the ruling elements, making Faro a particularly good bet for family beach vacations.

FARO TRAVEL GUIDE

Step away from the sand and you will find yourself wandering around the charming and compact old town. Lose yourself in the pedestrianized meandering streets paved with lovely mosaics and don't forget to take every chance you get to catch breath-taking views towards Faro's harbor. The historic center is endlessly alluring with its period architecture, landmark arches and the magnificent cathedral. What survives here stands as a proud and characterful testament to an oft-painful history, one marked by war tragedies and natural catastrophes.

The lagoon of Ria Formosa has been inhabited since the Paleolithic age. During the Roman occupation period, a settlement by the name of Ossonoba stood on the location of today's Faro and rose to importance due to its port, fishing and salt industry. A Moorish rule in the 8th

FARO TRAVEL GUIDE

century made Ossonoba a vital commercial town, with it briefly becoming a princedom capital in the 9th century.

It was around this time that a different name began being used for the town; called Santa Maria during the period, it later became known as Harun, which gave it its current name. The Moors left a profound mark in Faro's history up until their defeat by the Portuguese King Afonso III during the Reconquista in 1249, when the city became Algarve's most prominent one.

Sacked by the Earl of Essex in 1596 and reduced to shambles, it became secondary to Lagos which had already imposed itself as a capital. This lasted until the historic 1755 earthquake that heavily damaged most coastal towns with the exception of Faro. Although

FARO TRAVEL GUIDE

impacted as well, the town was protected by the sandy coast of the Ria Formosa lagoon and its superior sheltered position has lent it the administrative powers it still enjoys today.

Although chances are you will be tantalized enough by Faro to be content to stay here for the full course of your vacation, nearby attractions are sure to beckon you with their proximity and significance. Due to its location in the center of Algarve, Faro is a great base for those wanting to explore the wider region. Tour the magnificent beaches sprinkled around the Ria Formosa Nature Park, explore the ruins in close by Estoi and don't miss a chance to see the yachting lifestyle in the exclusive Vilamoura marina. Whatever you are looking for from your holiday, Faro is sure to deliver.

FARO TRAVEL GUIDE

🌎 Customs & Culture

The last town on the Iberian Peninsula to be liberated from Islamic rule, Faro's culture is invariably influenced by the diversity of peoples that have inhabited the area during its long history. A notable Moorish stamp is evident in landmarks and the general architecture of white-washed houses, with a certain feeling of an old world culture hard to brush off as you wander the maze of alleys in the center.

To begin to understand some of the history that sets the backbone to Faro's culture, pay attention to the ceramic tiles (*azulejos*) around the old town, which depict historic scenes and provide insight into the complexities of the town's past. Here, Baroque, Gothic and Renaissance styles converge into an architectural fusion, mirrored by

FARO TRAVEL GUIDE

the history of the city's most important landmarks; Faro's Cathedral, for example, has previously served as a Roman forum and subsequently a mosque.

For an in-depth coverage of the region's cultural heritage, check out the Municipal Museum chock-full of local ancient artifacts. Nearby Estoi with its Milreu Ruins is a magnet for history buffs where you can find one of the world's oldest churches. Additionally, whiffs of ancient Roman civilizations await you in the Cerro da Vila ruins in nearby Vilamoura.

If you are planning to travel to Faro during August, your visit may coincide with the annual FolkFaro festival (www.folkfaro.com) which takes place August 17-25. The festival is a colorful celebration of the region's folklore, but is also decidedly international, with performers, parades and various shows with worldwide participants.

🌍 Geography

The reason why Faro is a popular entry point for Algarve visitors is the proximity of the airport. At only 5 kilometers away from the city, Faro's airport (FAO) has witnessed a consistent increase of number of travelers, with low-cost airlines flocking to it in recent years.

Connected to the city center by bus and taxi, the airport is a mere 20-minute ride away (€2.20 by bus or about €10 by taxi)

Other options for arrival into Faro include a high-speed train from Lisbon (a 2.5 hour ride) as well as regional

FARO TRAVEL GUIDE

trains which connect it to other points along the Algarve coast.

Those wanting to discover the wider region should consider visiting with a vehicle (or hiring one), which will also enable you to explore at will. That being said, bus lines between Faro and a number of other cities on the Iberian Peninsula (including Lisbon, Porto, Madrid and Seville) run daily.

While walking within Faro is an enjoyable way to see the city, consider packing adequate footwear to avoid uncomfortable strolls around the cobblestone streets. If you are planning to use the public transportation within Faro, you should be looking out for buses number 14 and 16, which circulate around the city and travel as far as the

FARO TRAVEL GUIDE

airport and the Faro beach. Tickets can be bought on board and cost €2.20.

🌍 Weather & Best Time to Visit

A moderate Mediterranean climate, plenty of sunshine and a perpetual breeze make Faro a favorite destination year-round, with the Algarve winter being far from the gray and gloomy scenery found in European vacation spots further north.

Sunny days and temperatures averaging between 12 (54 °F) and 16 C (61 °F) are the norm here during winter, though you should be prepared for frequent rain if you choose to visit Faro in the off-season.

FARO TRAVEL GUIDE

Considered one of Europe's sunniest places, Faro's temperatures are pleasant throughout the year. But perhaps the best time to visit it is at very earliest of summer, when the air is still fresh but the sea is comfortably warm for a swim. Be prepared for a few colder nights up until June, and pack a change of warmer clothes just to be sure.

A lot of visitors prefer the months of July and August which can be considerably warmer and significantly busier. Average daily temperatures range between 27 and 35 °C (81–95 °F). But regardless of how hot it gets, the pleasant sea breezes are sure to help you keep your cool. The warm weather stretches well into fall, with October temperatures sometimes even approaching 30 C (85 °F).

FARO TRAVEL GUIDE

🌐 Money & Currency

The official currency in Portugal is the Euro. Prices encountered during your Faro holiday will vary depending on your choice of accommodation, entertainment and itinerary plans. However, as Faro is a working city and is often overlooked by tourists, prices here are generally more affordable than in other resorts around the Algarve. In fact, it has been voted as one of the most affordable European beach destinations, with fantastic value accommodation and eating options.

🌐 Maps

For an excellent and comprehensive map of Faro city centre, see:

http://www.farouncovered.com/Portals/Faro/map/map_faro.pdf

FARO TRAVEL GUIDE

Sights & Activities: What to See & Do

🌍 Old Town

The so-called Cidade Velha, Faro's old town, is a well-preserved historic section just to the east of the harbor. Winding cobblestone streets, Moorish-inspired architecture and a definitive sense of traveling back in time will make you want to wander around the 9th-century town for hours on end, marveling the lively mix of styles that has added multiple layers to Faro's character. Tragically, the historic center was burned down by the English troops in 1596 and then rebuilt only to be destroyed once again in the 1755 earthquake.

Remains surviving the Reconquista as well as the devastating earthquake today compete with 19th-century architecture in this delightful maze of alleys. Enter the city thought the significant 18th-century Arco de Villa arch and head towards the Faro Cathedral (Sé) on the orange tree-lined square. The nearby 18th-century Bishop's Palace is a good landmark to walk by before heading to the Municipal Museum where archeological relics unveil the city's long and eventful history.

To exit the historic center, go through the Arco da Porta Nova, a place where the old town meets the water and a departure point for boats heading to the Ria Formosa Natural Park.

Arco de Vila

An 18th-century gateway marking the entrance to the Cidade Velha, the Arco de Vila (Arch of the City) is a neoclassical arch built by the order of the Bishop Francisco Gomes. Designed by Francisco Xavier Fabri and constructed in 1812, the Arco de Vila sits on the site of a former medieval castle gate. With a Moorish portico and a strong brick-vaulted roof, the arch supports the statue of St. Thomas Aquinas (patron saint of Faro). Just above the gateway is the bell tower.

Walk towards the Largo da Sé Street opening up from the gate and you will soon catch a sign of the famous Sé Cathedral as well as the Bishop's Palace – two more landmarks closely most frequently associated with the city.

Cathedral

Largo da Sé, Faro

Tel: +351 289 806 632

Known simply as "Sé" among locals, the 13th-century Faro Cathedral dominates the old town district and is the area's crown jewel. Constructed on the site of a Roman forum turned into a Visigoth cathedral and later into a mosque, the Cathedral was completed in 1251 and its original exterior was clearly Romanesque-Gothic.

Largely rebuilt and renovated after the 1755 earthquake, its tower gate remains an original, as do several chapels. The renovation has resulted in a particularly varied mix of styles, including Baroque, Renaissance and Gothic, perfectly mirroring the city's eclectic collection of period architecture. And though its exterior may not be earth-shattering, the interior definitely is worth a peek; elaborate tiles and gilded carvings as well as a baroque organ are just some of the treasures found on the inside.

If you are on the hunt for spectacular views, make the effort to climb up to the rooftop lookout (*miradouro*) where you also may catch a glimpse of the storks that have made home in the bell towers. From here, you can get a bird's eye view of the typical Portuguese architecture present in Faro, including the iconic red rooftops called *tesouro* as well as the Ria Formosa Park with its magnificent lagoon.

The Cathedral is open daily from 09:00 to 12:30 and from 13:30 to 17:00 while Sunday mass is held at 10:00 and 12:00.

Admission costs €3. Entrance to the cathedral's gilded altar as well as the marbled tombs and chapels costs additional €3.

Bishop's Palace

Largo da Sé 15, Faro

Just opposite the Cathedral is the Bishop's Palace (Paco Episcopal), decorated in multicolored 18-th century hand-painted tiles (*azulejos*). With its red roof, it nowadays is a venue for various religious art exhibitions while its interior is a piece of art itself. The Palace was constructed at the site of the previous Episcopal residence, which was destroyed by the British troops in 1596. Rebuilt after the earthquake, its altarpiece was created in 1786.

Being still the official residence of the Bishop of Faro, the Palace is not open to the public but is nevertheless a lovely landmark to walk by. If your visit coincides with one of the occasional temporary exhibitions held here, you should use the opportunity to take a peek inside.

FARO TRAVEL GUIDE

Municipal Museum of Archeology

Largo Dom Afonso III, Faro

Tel: +351 289 897 400

Housed in one of Portugal's oldest convents – the 16th-century *Convento de Nossa Senhora da Assuncao* - the Municipal Museum of Archeology is one of Algarve's first museums. The museum surveys two millennia's worth of local history and art and is the proud home of the majestic Roman *Mosaic of the Ocean*, depicting Neptune and the Four Winds. Dating to the 3rd century, the mosaic was discovered in 1976 on a building site. A lovely cloister as well as other Roman and Moorish artifacts (both archeological and ecclesiastical) can also be found inside, including many relics excavated at the nearby Estoi site.

FARO TRAVEL GUIDE

The famous Faro-born painter Carlos Filipe Porfirio is represented with his moody paintings featuring local legends and religious motifs.

The Museum is open from 09:30 to 17:30 (from 11:30 on weekends) in the summer season and from 10:00 to 18:00 (from 14:00 on weekends) between the months of October and April. Admission fee costs €3 (€1.50 for students).

🌍 Ria Formosa Nature Park

Spanning about 60 kilometers of south Portugal's coastline, the Ria Formosa Natural Par was declared one of the country's great natural wonders and is an area of major ecological interest.

A lagoon formed by a sequence of sandpits (*Ilhas*) is the home of wetlands and has been protected since 1987. Unique natural conditions make it a breeding spot for birds, some of which are extremely rare, as well as a variety of marine life. At peak times in the winter season during migration, the park often hosts as many as 20,000 birds, with resident flamingos and the Purple Swamphen being the most recognizable species. A salt production site during Roman times, the landscape of the lagoon changes as one season gives way to the next, with parts of the park sometimes submerged and other times entirely exposed. Today, the area is used for oyster and mussel farming, mostly with the utilization of traditional methods in order to preserve the habitat.

Two peninsulas (Ancao and Cacela) as well as five islands (Barreta, Culatra, Armona, Tavira and Cabanas) make up the Ria Formosa Park. Accessible by small boats from the historic center, the Park can be visited as part of a two and a half hour boat trip (including a 40 minute stay on one of the islands), with prices starting from €10. Full day tours are also available and cost anywhere from €30 to €50 per adult, depending on the tour operator.

FARO TRAVEL GUIDE

🌐 Our Lady of Carmel Church & Chapel of Bones

Largo do Carmo, Faro

Tel: +351 289 824 490

Back to the mainland from the Ria Formosa Park and right at the exit of the old town, continue your Faro exploration by moving slightly inland. Just away from the town wall you will soon discover the baroque Igreja de Nossa Senhora do Carmo (Our Lady of Carmel Church). Started in 1713 and completed in 1719 during Joao V's rule, with its façade finished after the historic 1755 earthquake, this Carmelite church is extensively gilded with Brazilian gold in its interior and features imposing twin towers. It also contains significant religious statues, including the nine Triumphal Procession statues by

FARO TRAVEL GUIDE

Manuel Martins who also created the Santa Teresa altarpiece.

For those looking for something completely unusual and borderline bizarre, the 19th century Capela dos Ossos (Chapel of Bones) is a true find. The chapel is literally built from and decorated with the bones and skulls of 1,200 monks, all neatly arranged in rows. Completed in 1816, it is a peculiar work of art of the Carmelite monks who built it, inclined to use the remains of their predecessors from a nearby cemetery as a grim reminder of mortality. Entrance fee to this ghoulish chapel costs €1.

🌎 Beaches

When you acquainted yourself with Faro's history and culture, the logical choice is to head to one (or more) of the nearby exquisite beaches. Most of the beaches in and around Faro are located on the shallow pits of sand that run along the coastline. This natural landscape creates a

FARO TRAVEL GUIDE

wetland lagoon on the internal side, marked by calm and clear waters. The external, ocean-meeting side is somewhat wilder, with waves rolling in from the Atlantic.

Praia de Faro & Ilha de Faro

Faro's beach is a long, gently-sloping stretch of golden sand on Ilha de Faro (Faro Island), some 10 kilometers away from the city. Located on the sandbar that wraps around the coastline, it gets a bit crowded in July and August but nevertheless manages to please all tastes; with gorgeous views, a multitude of facilities and a wide range of entertainment options, it is truly the locals' favorite hangout in the summertime.

To get to the beach, take bus 14 or 16 from across the bus station in the city. The buses run about once every 30 minutes in the summertime and make a stop at the airport. The 45-minute journey itself is irresistibly scenic, particularly when crossing the pine forest region.

Ilha de Barreta/Deserta

Catch a ferry to Ilha de Barreta (also known as Ilha Deserta) to marvel at the long and narrow strip of sand just off the mainland and part of the Ria Formosa National Park. The sandpit that curves around the coast just in front of Faro can be accessed from various points on the mainland. The mind-blowing 10 kilometers of sweeping sands are connected to the wetlands where exotic flamingoes thrive so they provide a different experience from the one usually found on urban purposefully-organized beaches.

Ilha de Barreta is particularly well suited to explorers, with plenty of nature trails available for a change of pace from the more common beach activities. Note that only one restaurant serves the beach, so bringing a snack is recommended.

Vale de Lobo

If you head west of Faro, you will run into the popular Vale do Lobo resort whose dramatic Algarve-typical cliffs provide a stunning change of scenery. A wide beach awaits sun-worshipers, ready to provide its excellent facilities, cafes, bars and restaurants. Vale de Lobo's square (known as Praca) can be found right on the beach while those looking to explore further can head to the golf resort nearby.

Armona

One of the region's most popular beaches, Armona is located east of Faro about 2 kilometers off the Olhao coast and is accessible via ferry from Olhao or Fuseta. Endless sand stretches as far as the eye can reach, inviting leisurely strolls by the water's edge. The sand dunes in the background are home to a number of restaurants and bars while a camping site can also be found nearby.

🌍 Living Science Centre

Centro de Ciência Viva, Rua Comandante Francisco Manuel, Faro

Tel: +351 289 890 920

FARO TRAVEL GUIDE

http://www.ccvalg.pt

Faro's Living Science Centre is a great way to spend a day away from the beach, particularly for families with children. A place of learning and discovery, it features interactive exhibitions covering a multitude of areas, such as light, the solar system, and the human body, among others. Children's curious minds will have a chance to look at planets through a telescope or discover marine life with the use of microscopes. Permanent exhibitions dedicated to the sea as well as a flight simulator and astronomical observation sessions are just a few more of the many activities the whole family can engage in during the visit. Opened since 1997, the Living Science Centre is housed in the old fire station near the Manuel Bivar gardens. Entrance costs €3.50 for adults; €1.75 for children under 12.

🌍 Estoi & the Milreu Ruins

Just 11 kilometers north of Faro and set in the gorgeous countryside, Estoi is a quaint old town that easily justifies a half-day trip. A bus connects Faro and Estoi and drops visitors off in the main square, close to the 18th century pink rococo Palacio do Visconde de Estoi, nowadays a private palace. The Palace also features beautiful shaded gardens with tropic plants, open to the public.

Stroll downhill from the main square towards the 1st century Milreu Roman site and you will soon find the most compelling reason to visit Estoi - a locality that used to be inhabited between the 2nd and the 10th century, this is Algarve's most impressive and expansive Roman ruins site. Built in the style of a peristyle villa (a columned porch surrounding a court), it features intact columns and original mosaics. A temple originally devoted to the cult of water, then converted to a basilica in the 3rd century

AD, is one of the world's oldest churches. The remains of a bathing complex have also withheld the test of time, and feature fish mosaics in the bathrooms and an intricate changing room including a *frigidarium* designed to hold cold water. The villa used to feature an advanced water supply network as well as heated rooms and thermal springs.

Check out the amusing decorations found around the ruins, with fish represented as particularly fat in order to create the optical illusion of movement, testifying to the level of dedication to detail and effort put into the creation of this ancient villa.

Entrance into the ruins costs €2 and they are open from 10:30 to 13:00 and from 14:00 to 18:30 daily between May and September; 09:30 to 13:00 and 14:00 to 17:00 the rest of the year.

🌍 Tavira

Another popular day trip out of Faro is Tavira, one of Algarve's prettiest towns. Only 30 kilometers east of Faro

FARO TRAVEL GUIDE

and sitting on both sides of the Gilao River, this traditional fishing town was founded as early as 4th century BC and served as a port for trading with North Africa. Tavira is a popular destination not only for its picturesque beauty defined by graceful 18th-century houses, palm trees and low bridges, but also because of the spectacular beach on Ilha de Tavira.

Roman Bridge

Today's bridge being mostly built in 1667 on top of a previous structure, the Roman Bridge was initially constructed during the Islamic al-Andalus rule in Tavira. A vital factor in the defense system of medieval Tavira, it used to have houses erected on it as it connected the two banks of the River Gilao. Collapsing in 1655, it was rebuilt about a decade later, largely featuring today's characteristics.

Partially destroyed once again in the 1989 flood but quickly restored, it is no longer used for motor vehicle traffic and is fully pedestrianized, thus inviting a leisurely stroll.

An interesting detail worth noting is the fact that the river to the west of the bridge is known as Gilao while the very same river goes by the name Sequa to east; the reason can be found in a complex local legend that involves two lovers who had tragically drowned on either side of the bridge.

Tavira Island

Easily accessible from the town of Tavira via a ferry, the Ilha de Tavira (Tavira Island) stretches out towards the southwest and is a giant 14-kilometers-long beach with spectacular dunes in the background. Its width varies between 150 meters and 1 kilometer, making it seem truly endless at times. Likely one of Algarve's best beaches, it is typically flocked to in the summertime but it is relatively easy to steer clear of the crowds on such a large stretch. Even naturists can find spots specifically designed for them on Ilha de Tavira. Bars and restaurants cater to travelers' every needs as does the variety of beach sceneries – those looking for more tranquil waters should head to the lagoon-facing side, while those not intimidated by waves will delight if they choose the Atlantic-facing orientation.

Tavira's blue flag beach can be accessed from the mainland (Quatro Aguas) via frequent ferries (from €1.50 round trip) or water taxis (from €20). If you are charmed by the beach and wish to spend a night on Tavira Island, look into the camping site under the pine trees – the only available overnight accommodation on the Ilha de Tavira.

🌎 Vilamoura

Vilamoura is a luxurious tourist resort and the largest complex of its kind in Europe. Stretching over an area of 20 km², it was built with a purpose to accommodate a variety of tastes and is most notably known for its marina, golf course complexes and a dense population of hotels. For those looking for a bit of history and culture, the nearby Cerro da Vila ruins are a logical choice as they are one of the most significant archeological sites in the country.

Vilamoura is located 23 kilometers west of Faro and is accessible via bus (€4 one way) or taxi (starting from €27 one way).

Vilamoura Marina

Vilamoura

Tel: +351 289 310 560

http://www.marinadevilamoura.com/en

The main center of activity in Vilamoura, the marina is alive with restaurants, bars and shops, some of which are decidedly upscale. This is Portugal's largest marina and is sure to keep you entertained for hours. Peaceful during the day and pulsing with life at night, it attracts everyday folk as well as the wealthy and the popular.

With a capacity to berth more than 1,000 boats, it sees a lot of yacht traffic and also provides options for chartering boats.

Water sports activities are frequently organized as well, and include deep-sea fishing, cruises and scuba diving. The marina was recently voted Best Portuguese Marina for 2013 and certainly makes Vilamoura a particularly cosmopolitan destination along the Algarve coast.

Cerro da Vila

Avenida Cerro Da Vila, 8125-403 Vilamoura

Tel: +351 289 312 153

Just steps from the marina, the Cerro da Vila ruins with leftovers from ancient civilizations are a great way to spend a few more hours in Vilamoura. The particular site has been occupied since the Bronze Age but the earliest settlers were the Romans who have left an unmistakable mark on the area, mostly between the 2nd and 3rd century AD. Cerro da Vila then belonged to the Ossonoba province and served the lands around the settlement with its port.

Remnants of a rustic mansion (Roman Villa), public bathhouses and fish salting tanks can be found on this ruins complex, as well as foundations of a tower used for burials. The area is nowadays an archeological site of immense importance in Algarve. A museum has been created within the complex, to serve as a guide to visitors wanting to further explore the significance of the site. The ruins are open from 10:00 to 13:00 and from 16:00 to 21:00 in the summertime. Between the months of November and April you can visit the Cerro da Villa from 09:30 to 12:30 or from 14:00 to 18:00. Entrance to the site costs €5.

Budget Tips

🌐 Accommodation

Casa d'Alagoa Hostel

Praca Alexandre Herculano 27, 8000-160 Faro

Tel: +351 289 813 252

http://farohostel.com/

If you don't mind staying in a hostel, consider the

FARO TRAVEL GUIDE

historical Casa d'Alagoa – an affordable accommodation in central Faro that is sure to please a range of tastes.

Both private and shared rooms are available in this excellently located and clean hostel just across the Alagoa garden, with great connections to Faro's beaches. One can also easily reach the historic Arco da Vila in only 5 minutes on foot.

The high-ceilinged rooms come equipped with Wi-Fi, a buffet breakfast and the use of a convenient communal kitchen. Laundry services and bike rentals are also available through the staff reception desk.

FARO TRAVEL GUIDE

At the start of the summer season, private bathroom double rooms start from €48 per night, including breakfast while beds in shared dormitories start from €17 per night.

Hotel Ibis Faro

Estrada Nacional 125, 8000-770 Faro

Tel: +351 289 893 800

http://www.ibis.com/gb/hotel-1593-ibis-faro/index.shtml

Just two kilometers from Faro's center, the Hotel Ibis Faro – part of the Ibis chain of hotels – is perfectly located for easy access to the nearby beaches, the Ria Formosa Natural Park and the historic center with its landmarks. The hotel's 81 rooms all include Wi-Fi access and are simply decorated, with private bathrooms and A/C. An outdoor swimming pool and a bar with a terrace are available for hotel's guests as is the private parking. Golf lovers should know that the nearest course is merely 10 kilometers away.

Double rooms in the early summer season (June) start from €49 per night, with an optional breakfast price of €6 per person per night.

Hotel Adelaide

Rua Cruz das Mestras n 9, 8000-261 Faro

Tel: +351 289 802

http://www.adelaideresidencial.net

For another affordable option in central Faro, travelers should look into the 2-star Hotel Adelaide – a 19-room hotel within walking distance of the Faro bus station and the marina. Rooms are bright and offer free Wi-Fi and air-conditioning while the hotel also has a restaurant serving daily buffet breakfast. Shared kitchen facilities are also available for use by hotel's guests.

The 19 double rooms in the Adelaide are available at rates starting at €50 per night in the mid-season, breakfast included.

Hotel Faro

Praça D. Francisco Gomes, N 2, 8000 -168 Faro

Tel: +351 289 830 830

http://www.hotelfaro.pt/

If you are looking for affordable accommodation right in the middle of Faro's center, look no further than Hotel Faro, a 4-star choice overlooking the old town and the marina. Large and bright rooms come with cable TV, a minibar and private bathrooms, while some also include balconies. A buffet breakfast is optional and a restaurant on the rooftop serves Portuguese cuisine as well.

Prices for one of Hotel Faro's 90 rooms start from €75 for a double room in the mid-season, breakfast included.

Quinta dos Poetas, Hotel Rural Olhao

Sítio da Arretorta, 8700-180 Olhão

Tel: + 351 289 990 990

http://www.quintadospoetas.com/

Outside Faro and in located in Olhao's countryside, the Hotel Rural Quinta dos Poetas is set against picturesque scenery. Providing 22 rooms with private balconies, air-condition and wooden furniture, the hotel also offers a pool, a fitness room and a local cuisine restaurant.

Renting a bicycle to explore the nearby Ria Formosa is easy and is a great option for nature lovers. Free private parking is also available on the hotel's grounds.

Double rooms with breakfast in the early summer season start at €75 per night.

🌐 Restaurants, Cafés & Bars

Columbus Cocktail and Wine Bar

Praca Dom Francisco Gomes, 13, Faro

Tel: +351 917 762 22

FARO TRAVEL GUIDE

http://www.barcolumbus.pt/

Head here right before dinner for a glass of perfect sangria or for a delicious cocktail afterwards. Columbus Bar, located just across from the marina, is a favorite with locals and tourists alike and serves a wide range of excellent cocktails on a nice terrace.

A stylish bar inside is another option for visitors and the attentive staff also serves delicious tapas. Cocktails cost about €6 and some of the more popular ones include the Strawberry Daiquiri and the Cosmopolitan. The clientele is varied at this popular bar, with hordes of repeat visitors coming in from all over Algarve.

FARO TRAVEL GUIDE

Tasca do Ricky

Rua do Forno, N021, Faro

Tel: +351 919 111 057

This typical Portuguese tasca (small restaurant) is a great choice for a filling and affordable lunch, with a large portion main dish, dessert, drink and coffee setting you back a mere €6. Home-cooked food and a very friendly service are Ricky's trademark as the owner is known to personally greet patrons at the door. Don't ask for a menu; simply follow his instructions as he guides you through what is at its best and freshest that day. The restaurant is closed on Sunday evenings.

Jamie's Faro

Largo de Sao Pedro 54, Faro

Tel: +351 961 480 083

http://www.jamiesfaro.com/

Definitely one of the more popular restaurants in the city, Jamie's Faro offers excellent value for money. Located near the Chapel of Bones, it features a lovely terrace providing a relaxed setting for al-fresco dining as well as impeccable service by the courteous staff. The menu of the day costs just under €9 and includes a dish (selected from four options), drink and coffee. Try the risotto with grilled stuffed chicken and the exquisite chocolate mousse and don't skip a glass of the excellent house white wine.

Adega Nova

Rua Francisco Barreto, 24, Faro

Tel: +351 289 813 433

The rustic and informal Adega Nova serves quality food which changes ever so slightly day by day. Try the Algarve cheese as a starter and continue on to sample delightful fresh seafood such as octopus with rice or the mixed seafood skewer (€13). Wash it all down with the young sparkling wine Vinho Verde as you chat with the locals sitting on the next table for a true cultural immersion experience.

Atelier de Comida Sto Antonio

Largo de Camoes 23/24, Faro

Tel: +351 289 802 148

FARO TRAVEL GUIDE

http://www.atelierdecomida.com/

Excellent food and wine await you in the Atelier de Comida Sto Antonio and you will soon realize that the restaurant is packed with locals – always a good sign. The backyard is a lovely setting for outdoor dining in the summertime. Competitively priced and delicious dishes include monkfish shish-kebab (€12.50), sauteed sea bream (€12.50), bacon-wrapped sea bass (€13.50) and pork tenderloin with clams (€11.50), to name just a few. Takeaway options are also available, with the soup of the day particularly well priced at only €1.

Shopping

Forum Algarve

Forum Algarve EN 125 Km 103, Faro

Tel: +351 289 889 300

http://www.forumalgarve.net/

The Forum Algarve shopping mall, located on the main EN125 road, has a wide selection of shops, restaurants and cafes and an open air central square. Shopping aficionados will delight at the more than 100 stores spanning a wide range of goods (including fashion, cosmetics, home ware, books, gifts and a good selection of services). There is also a cinema complex in the Forum, a large supermarket as well as over 20 different restaurant and café establishments. The Forum Algarve is easibly accessible by public minibus transport which runs every 15 minutes.

Mercado Municipal de Faro

Largo Doutor Francisco Sá Carneiro, Faro

Tel: +351 289 897 250

http://www.mercadomunicipaldefaro.pt

If you are on the hunt for fresh produce or simply want to mingle with the locals, head to the Mercado Municipal where countless stalls will delight you with the freshest of ingredients and their varied offerings. The indoor market is a heaven for foodies and those looking to stock up on food gifts (such as salty olives and cured meats) all at amazingly low prices. For a sweet treat while you shop, try the delicious custard tarts.

FARO TRAVEL GUIDE

Carminho

Rua Santo António 29, Faro

Tel: +351 289 826 522

Most of Faro's shopping can be found along the Rua Santo Antonio street right in the center of the city. If you have souvenir shopping to do, check out the Carminho store where handicrafts and some traditional Portuguese attire await you. Traditional painted *azulejos*, tableware, embroidery and items made of copper are just a few more of the products on sale at the well-stocked Carminho.

Garrafeira Rui

Praça Ferreira de Almeida, 28, 8000 Faro

Tel: +351 289 822 803

If you have, like many others before you, fallen in love with delicious Portuguese wines, head to the Garrafeira Rui – Faro's best known wine shop. Here you can stock up on local wines and port as well as purchase local delicacies, such as sausages, cheeses and sweets. The store is open Monday to Saturday from 08:00 to 20:00.

Estoi Flea Market

If you can time your visit to Estoi to coincide with the 2nd Sunday of the month, take advantage of the large open air market where traders from all over the region congregate to sell produce, clothing, antiques and a large selection of handmade crafts. Items worth hunting for here include hats and baskets woven from palm leaves – one of Algarve's most popular souvenirs.

FARO TRAVEL GUIDE

Know Before You Go

🌍 Entry Requirements

By virtue of the Schengen agreement, travellers from other countries in the European Union do not need a visa when visiting Portugal. Travellers from the UK, Bulgaria, Croatia, Cyprus, Romania and Ireland are also exempted from needing a visa and visitors from Australia, Canada and the USA, do not require a visa, provided that their stay does not exceed 90 days. Travellers requiring a Schengen visa will be able to enter Portugal with it multiple times within a 6 month period, if their stay does not exceed 90 days. They may need to prove that they have sufficient funds available to cover the duration of their stay in Portugal. For a stay exceeding 90 days, non-EU visitors will need to apply for a temporary residence permit.

🌍 Health Insurance

Citizens of other EU countries as well as residents from Switzerland, Norway, Iceland and Liechtenstein and the UK are covered for health care in Portugal with the European Health Insurance Card (EHIC), which can be applied for free of charge. If you need a Schengen visa for your stay in Portugal, you will also be required to obtain proof of health insurance for the duration of your stay (that offers at least €37,500 coverage), as part of their visa application. Visitors from Canada or the USA should check whether their regular health insurance covers travel and arrange for extended health insurance if required.

🌐 Travelling with Pets

When travelling with pets from another country in the European Union, certain requirements have to be met. The animal will need to be microchipped and up to date on their rabies shots. Additionally you should have applied for a EU pet passport from your country of origin. If you are planning to visit Portugal from outside the European Union, a health certificate in English or Portuguese needs to be submitted by a certified vet. For the non-commercial transport of animals to Portugal from non-European Union countries, the relevant authority at the Portuguese point of entry needs to be informed in writing at least 48 hours in advance of the arrival of the animal.

🌐 Airports

Apart from the airports in Lisbon, Faro and Oporto, Portugal's busiest routes are to the islands of the Azores and the Canaries. **Lisbon Portela Airport** (LIS) is the busiest international airport in Portugal and connects travellers with its capital,

FARO TRAVEL GUIDE

Lisbon. **Francisco de Sá Carneiro Airport** (OPO) near Oporto is Portugal's second busiest airport. It is a focus city for EasyJet and Ryanair. **Faro Airport** (FAO) is particularly busy during the summer months, when it provides access to the Algarve region. **Madeira Airport** (FNC), with its notoriously short runway, was once considered one of the most dangerous airports. Located in Santa Cruz near Funchal, it provides access to the island of Madeira from destinations in France, Germany, Finland, the Netherlands and the UK. Another important airport in the Azores is **Horta International Airport** (HOR), which provides a vital link to the archipelago's outlying islands, such as Flores and Corvo. **Santa Maria Airport** (SMA) on the island of Santa Maria in the Azores once served as an important hub for the facilitation of trans-Atlantic connections, particularly in the post-World War Two era. Although it has in recent years slipped into a more regional role, it still has amenities suitable for transatlantic aircraft.

Airlines

TAP Portugal is the flag-carrying airline of Portugal. Founded in 1946, it flies travellers to 88 different destinations in 38 countries including Amsterdam, Barcelona, Madrid, Berlin, Frankfurt, Munich, Oslo, Marrakech, Miami, Luanda, Maputo, Moscow, Casablanca, Panama and Rio de Janeiro. SATA Air

Açores is a small airline based in the Azores, which operates scheduled flights as a carrier of passengers, cargo and mail. In the late 1990s, it acquired OceanAir and renamed it SATA International. Sata provides scheduled flights connecting Ponta Delgada to Lisbon, Madeira Island and Porto and also operates trans-Atlantic routes to Faro and Toronto. Portugalia began operations as a regional airline in the 1980s, flying domestic routes within Portugal as well as to Italy, France, Spain, Germany and Morocco. It was acquired by TAP Portugal in 2006.

Lisbon Portela Airport serves as a hub for Portugalia and TAP Portugal, as well as White Airlines, which operates mainly chartered flights on behalf of Portuguese tour operators. It is also a focus city for EasyJet and Ryanair. SATA Air Açores and SATA International are based at João Paulo II Airport in the Azores.

Currency

The currency of Portugal is the Euro. It is issued in notes in denominations of €500, €200, €100, €50, €20, €10 and €5. Coins are issued in denominations of €2, €1, 50c, 20c, 10c, 5c, 2c and 1c.

FARO TRAVEL GUIDE

🌐 Banking & ATMs

Using ATMs in Portugal to withdraw money is simple if your ATM card is compatible with the MasterCard/Cirrus or Visa/Plus networks. Portuguese ATM machines are also known as Multibanco and will be identified with the logo, MB. There is a good distribution of machines available throughout Portugal. In general ATMs will give you the most beneficial rate of exchange, although some bank groups may levy an additional fee on international transactions. European ATMs are configured for 4-digit PIN numbers.

🌐 Credit Cards

Visa and MasterCard are widely accepted in many Portuguese businesses. Some businesses also accept American Express and will indicate this by displaying its logo. Other credit cards valid in Portugal include Diners Club, Maestro, Europay and JCB. Credit cards issued in Europe are smart cards that that are fitted with a microchip and require a PIN for each transaction. If you still have an older magnetic strip card, you may find that some facilities are not configured to process your transaction. Do remember to advise your bank or credit card company of your travel plans before leaving home.

🌍 Tourist Taxes

The city of Lisbon introduced a tourist tax in 2015 which will charge visitors €1 per night for the first 7 days of their stay in Lisbon. The tax does not apply to minor children. A review of this policy is due in 2019.

🌍 Reclaiming VAT

If you are not from the European Union, you can claim back VAT (Value Added Tax) paid on your purchases in Portugal. The VAT rate in Portugal is 23 percent and this can be claimed back on your purchases, if certain conditions are met. Only purchases of €60 and over qualify for a VAT refund. You will be asked for proof (usually in the form of a passport) that your normal residence is outside the European Union. Participating shops will clearly display that they offer a VAT-free service. A form needs to be filled in by the shop assistant. At customs of your last port within the European Union (which need not be the place where you bought the goods), you should submit this form. The goods and sales invoice will be inspected before the form is stamped and approved.

🌐 Tipping Policy

A service fee is usually included in restaurant bills in Portugal, but it is accepted to leave an additional 5-10 percent gratuity. It is also customary to tip taxi drivers 5 to 10 percent of the fee.

🌐 Mobile Phones

Most EU countries, including Portugal uses the GSM mobile service. This means that most UK phones and some US and Canadian phones and mobile devices will work in Portugal. However, phones using the CDMA network will not be compatible. While you could check with your service provider about coverage before you leave, using your own service in roaming mode will involve additional costs. The alternative is to purchase a Portuguese SIM card to use during your stay in Portugal. Portugal has three mobile networks. They are MEO (formerly known as TMN), Vodafone and NOS (formerly known as Optimus). MEO is the largest service provider that offers the best coverage and SIM cards are available from €2.50. Data only rates begin at €10 for 10GB, valid for 3 days. Vodafone has a vendor at Porto airport and you can get a data only SIM card for €2.50 or voice and data. The data rate begins at €1.99 for 100 Mb. Bear in mind that for the data only package there are two different rates, a 7 day rate and a 30 day rate, which cannot be interchanged. NOS is the smallest of the Portuguese networks. They offer a SIM card for €2.50, with various top-up packages ranging from €1.99 for 30 MB that expires within 24 hours to €7.99 for 1 GB that is valid for one month.

Dialling Code

The international dialling code for Portugal is +351.

Emergency Numbers

Police: 112

Medical Emergencies: 112

Fire Rescue: 112

Forest Fires: 117

24 Hour Health line for emergencies: 808 242 424

Sea Rescue: 214 401 919

Maritime Police: 210 911 100

MasterCard: 800 811 272

Visa: 800 811 107

FARO TRAVEL GUIDE

🌐 Public Holidays

1 January: New Year's Day

March/April: Good Friday

25 April: Freedom Day

1 May: Worker's Day

10 June: Portugal Day

15 August: Feast of the Assumption

8 December: Immaculate Conception

25 December: Christmas Day

🌐 Time Zone

In the winter season from the end of October to the end of March, Portugal's official time is the same as Greenwich Mean Time/Coordinated Universal Time (GMT/UTC); Eastern Standard Time (North America) -4; Pacific Standard Time (North America) -7.

🌐 Daylight Savings Time

Clocks are set forward one hour on the last Sunday of March and set back one hour on the last Sunday of October for Daylight Savings Time.

🌐 School Holidays

The academic year in Portugal begins in mid September and ends in mid June, but there may be different schedules for private and international schools. The summer holiday is from mid June to mid September, although the exact times may vary according to region. There are short breaks between Christmas and New Year and also during Easter and for the Carnival season in February or March.

🌐 Trading Hours

Most shops in Portugal trade from 9am to 7pm on weekdays and until 1pm on Saturdays, but at some shopping centers, trading hours may be extended to midnight. Shops may also stay open on Saturday afternoons and even Sundays during the Christmas season. Certain shops close for lunch between 1 and 3pm. Banks are open from 8.30am to 3pm on weekdays and the post office is open from 9am to 6pm, Monday to Friday, with extended weekend hours available in at some branches, for example at the airport. Pharmacies trade from 9am to 7pm, but details about the nearest all night pharmacy will usually also be signposted.

FARO TRAVEL GUIDE

🌐 Driving Laws

The Portuguese drive on the right hand side of the road. A driver's licence from any of the European Union member countries is valid in Portugal. If visiting from a non-EU country, you will need to obtain an International Driving Permit to be able to drive in Portugal. The minimum driving age in Portugal is 18. The speed limit in Portugal is 120km per hour for freeways, 90km per hour for rural roads and 50km per hour in urban areas. The alcohol limit in Portugal is below 0.5 g/l. Toll roads in Portugal can be paid at dispensing booths or alternately, you could obtain a permanent or temporary electronic device that will be identified as a toll pass. This can be paid via credit card or ATM. Children under the age of 12 are not allowed to ride in the front seat. It is also illegal to drive with head phones or when using a mobile phone. Make sure that the vehicle you are using is up to date on road tax, fully covered by third party insurance and carries standard emergency gear such as warning triangles and a reflective safety vest. If older than four years, the car needs to have a valid IPO (Inspecção Periódica Obrigatória) as proof of roadworthiness.

🌐 Drinking Laws

In Portugal, the legal purchase age is 16 for beer and wine and 18 for spirits. The sale of alcohol in bars and restaurants is forbidden after midnight and public drinking after 2am.

🌐 Smoking Laws

In 2008, smoking was banned in all public places in Portugal, including work spaces, public transport, schools, libraries, museums, indoor car parks, indoor sports facilities, bars, cafes and discos. Restaurants with a floor space exceeding 100 sq. m. can allocate an enclosed area of not more than 30 percent with adequate ventilation as a smoker's area. The minimum age for smoking is 18. Persons who violate anti-smoking laws can be liable for a fine of between €50 and €750.

🌐 Electricity

Electricity: 230 volts
Frequency: 50 Hz
Portuguese electricity sockets are compatible with the Type C Euro adaptor and Type F plugs, which features two round pins or prongs. If travelling from the USA, you will need a power converter or transformer to convert the voltage from 230 to 110,

to avoid damage to your appliances. The latest models of many laptops, camcorders, mobile phones and digital cameras are dual-voltage with a built in converter.

🌎 Tourist Information (TI)

There are several tourist information outlets in Lisbon, the capital. The Lisbon Welcome Center is at 15 Rua do Arsenal, but there is also a tourist information outlet at Lisbon Portela Airport and Palacio Foz, in Praca dos Restauradores. The Cascais tourist information office is at Rua Visconde da Luz and there is also a tourist information outlet at Avenue Miguel Bombarda in Sintra. The Porto Convention Bureau at Ponte Luís I promotes tourism in Porto.

🌎 Food & Drink

Fish and seafood are important ingredients of Portuguese cuisine. One of the most popular dishes is bacalhau or salted cod, which can be found in a huge selection of regional varieties. Sardines - grilled or fried, is another national favorite and makes common street food in Lisbon, particularly in June when the Santa Antonio festival takes place. The traditional Portuguese soup is Caldo Verde, with a base of onion and potato and another signature dish is feijoada, a rich and meaty bean stew. Chouriço is a Portuguese pork sausage similar to the Spanish chorizo and it has a kosher counterpart in alheira de mirandela. Originally devised by Iberian Jews to fool the Inquisitors, the sausage may include veal, rabbit, chicken and duck.

Try Caldeirada de Enguias or eel stew from Aveiro or the seafood stew cataplana from the Algarve. In Porto, try the francesinha, a sandwich stuffed with ham, sausage and steak, smothered in cheese and then served with a signature tomato based sauce. The island of Madeira has plenty to offer, gastronomically speaking, ranging from meaty Espetada to Bolo de Mel or honey cake. The Azores boasts a selection of dairy products, including the well-known Queijo da Ilha which originates from the island, São Jorge. Here, too, seafood is popular, particularly octopus, mackerel and lamprey. Enjoy home-grown pineapples and the one-pot speciality cozida on São Miguel, while a slow-cooked Alcatra pot-roast may tantalize your taste buds on Terçeira. Azorean sweets include Massa Sovada or Portuguese sweet bread, and Malasadas.

Port wine, also known as Vinho de Porto, is a sweet, fortified wine made of red grapes grown exclusively in the Douro Valley of northern Portugal. It is traditionally enjoyed after dinner and served with cheese. Madeira is famous for wines such as Bual, Sercial, Malmsey and Verdelho. You should also try Poncho, a drink made from sugarcane rum, lemon juice and honey or ginja, a local liqueur distilled from cherries. Nikita, a blend of pineapple and vanilla can be enjoyed with or without alcohol. Try the distinctive wines from São Miguel and Pico in the Azores.

🌐 Websites

https://www.visitportugal.com/en

http://portugal.com/

http://wikitravel.org/en/Portugal

http://www.insideportugaltravel.com/

http://www.portugal-live.com/

http://www.portugal-live.net/

http://www.travel-in-portugal.com/

Printed in Great Britain
by Amazon